WASTE, RECYCLING AND RE-USE

Steve Parker

**RAINTREE
STECK-VAUGHN
PUBLISHERS**
The Steck-Vaughn Company

Austin, Texas

PROTECTING OUR PLANET

FORESTS FOR THE FUTURE

FUELS FOR THE FUTURE

KEEPING THE AIR CLEAN

KEEPING WATER CLEAN

THE WORLD'S WILD PLACES

WASTE, RECYCLING AND RE-USE

Published by Raintree Steck-Vaughn Publishers,
an imprint of Steck-Vaughn Company

Library of Congress Cataloging-in-Publication Data
Parker, Steve.
Waste, recycling and re-use/ Steve Parker.
    p.   cm.—(Protecting our planet)
    Includes bibliographical references and index.
    Summary: Discusses efforts to save the environment
    through recycling and waste management.
    ISBN 0-8172-4940-0
    1. Refuse and refuse disposal—Juvenile literature.
    2.Recycling (Waste, etc.)—Juvenile literature.
    [1. Refuse and refuse disposal. 2. Recycling (waste)]
    I. Title. II. Series.
    TD792.P37 1998
    363.7—dc21   97-29907

Printed in Italy. Bound in the United States.
1 2 3 4 5 6 7 8 9 0 02 01 00 99 98

CONTENTS

WASTED OPPORTUNITIES

We live in a wasteful world. There are trash cans and bulging black plastic bags in houses, schools, offices, factories, and public places. Vast areas of land are covered with garbage dumps. Waste gases and chemicals pour out of vehicle exhausts and industrial chimneys into the air. Liquid waste from factories streams out of pipes into rivers, lakes, and seas. In some places, the world seems to be filling up with waste.

WASTE IN TIME AND PLACE

Is waste simply something that you do not want? Not exactly.

- You may not want those old newspapers. But the collector for the local paper recycling center certainly does.

- You may not want those old-looking, grubby plates. But in a few years someone might recognize them as valuable antiques and clean and sell them.

- You may not want an old black-and-white, small-screen television. But someone in another, poorer country might be very pleased to have any kind of TV at all.

Waste varies with people, time, and place.

▼ This huge mound of waste took lots of energy, raw materials, and time to create. Now it is useless.

▲ The waste chemicals in these drums must be carefully disposed of or they will cause pollution.

WHAT IS WASTE?

Different countries and governments have various definitions of waste. These are usually very lengthy and complicated. Since 1994 a common definition of waste has been "any substance or object... which the producer or the person in possession of it discards." But then we must explain "discard"—"a substance or object that has been discarded is no longer part of the normal commercial cycle or chain of utility."

In other words, there isn't a simple definition. For the purposes of this book, waste will be defined as "something that has been thrown away because the person who owns it doesn't want it, can't use it, or can't sell it."

TYPES OF WASTE

Waste takes many forms and types. Waste can be grouped by where it comes from. Domestic waste from homes, municipal waste from public areas and facilities, industrial waste from factories, and agricultural waste from farming are all examples of waste.

Alternatively, waste can be grouped by the main substances and materials in it. Biodegradable or organic waste, like leftover foods and most types of paper and cardboard, will decay and eventually return to the soil and nature. Nonbiodegradable waste, which generally comes from manufacturing and industry, is a much bigger problem. It includes glass, metal, and plastic.

BURIED BY WASTE

By the year 2030, there could be 10 billion people in the world. If they all produce solid waste at the mid-1990s U.S. rate, the amount will be 400 billion tons—enough to bury all of Los Angeles to a depth of more than 300 ft. (100 m).

A DISPOSABLE WORLD

Long ago, when there were no people on Earth, there was no waste either. Nature wastes nothing and recycles everything. Dead trees are not waste—they gradually rot back into the soil, providing nutrients for new plants to grow. Likewise, animal droppings are not waste—they rot away, too, or they are consumed by hordes of maggots, worms, beetles, and other excrement eaters. These, in turn, become food for other creatures, and so on.

▲ The housefly may be a pest for humans. In the wild, its eggs hatch into maggots that eat rotting flesh—part of nature's recycling system.

A BRIEF HISTORY OF WASTE

Then came people. Some of our first wastes were piles of stone tools, bones, and ashes from the bodies of animals butchered and cooked on cave fires. Human numbers increased, and our industries and technologies advanced. People began mining ore rocks and heating them to obtain metals such as bronze, copper, and iron and firing clays to make cups, bowls, and utensils. Mine spoil, spent fuels, furnace slag, and burned-out ovens became concentrated, less natural waste.

When the Industrial Revolution began in the eighteenth century, more people were able to buy more possessions and inventions, which were being churned out by more factories—producing more waste.

MORE COMFORT AND PLEASURE

At the start of the twentieth century came bigger factories, making ever more complex items such as telephones, radios, cars, and washing machines. Great advances in technology and manufacturing made life safer, more comfortable, and pleasurable —although only for some people, mainly in developed, industrialized nations.

A CITY'S INS AND OUTS

"A European city with one million inhabitants requires, on average, more than 10,000 tons of fossil fuels, more than 300,000 tons of water, and 2,000 tons of food, and it converts these into 1,500 tons of harmful emissions, 300,000 tons of waste water and 1,600 tons of solid waste. And this happens every day."
—Dr. Klaus Topfer, former German environmental minister

▼ Technology changes so quickly that computers, TVs, and similar electronic equipment become outdated in a few years.

THE WASTE EXPLOSION

Today, there are twice as many people in the world as there were 100 years ago. Most want comfortable lifestyles with the newest labor-saving appliances, latest fashions, fast foods, less work and worry, and more time, leisure, money, and fun. The "old" has become even more useless and boring, thrown away for the "new."

The throwaway attitude is encouraged by advertising on television, and in magazines and other media, which tells us we must have the latest and newest. Giant manufacturing businesses want to make big profits, by selling more and more goods. People in less developed countries see the high standard of living in rich nations, and naturally they want the same. Because there are more people, and each person buys far more goods than ever before, there is much more waste.

▲ These paper plates and hats will be used once and thrown away, so it is important that they are recycled.

DOMESTIC WASTE

What have you put in the garbage can this week? Wrappers, last week's magazines, throwaway leaflets, fruit pits and cores, bits of old food, socks with holes, maybe an old battery, even an unwanted toy or a broken gadget like a personal stereo. In an average Western household, the weight of the weekly garbage builds up as in the graph opposite.

WHO MAKES MOST WASTE?

Householders in rich, industrial countries such as the United States, Japan, and Germany produce most waste. For most types of waste, the U.S. city dweller is in the lead, responsible for 4.5–6.5 lbs. (2–3 kg) every day. People in rural South America, Africa, or Asia produce much less.

▲ In most cities, garbage collection is very costly and labor intensive. It involves hundreds of workers and dozens of vehicles on the streets.

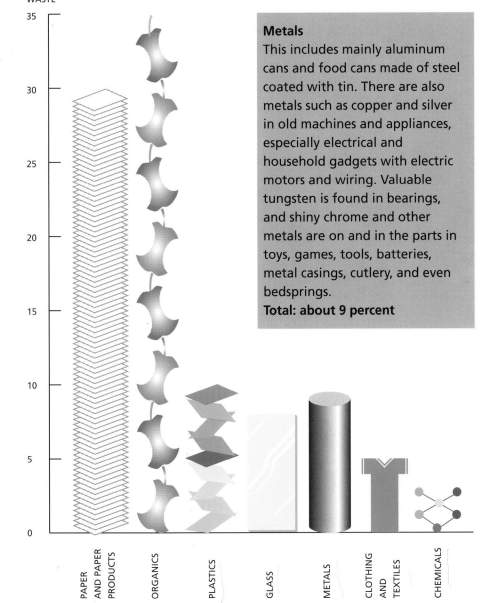

% OF DOMESTIC WASTE

35

30

25

20

15

10

5

0

PAPER AND PAPER PRODUCTS | ORGANICS | PLASTICS | GLASS | METALS | CLOTHING AND TEXTILES | CHEMICALS

Metals
This includes mainly aluminum cans and food cans made of steel coated with tin. There are also metals such as copper and silver in old machines and appliances, especially electrical and household gadgets with electric motors and wiring. Valuable tungsten is found in bearings, and shiny chrome and other metals are on and in the parts in toys, games, tools, batteries, metal casings, cutlery, and even bedsprings.
Total: about 9 percent

Organics—food scraps, leftovers, and yard waste
These include food waste such as vegetable peelings, and yard waste.
Total: about 35 percent

Plastics
The list of plastic waste is very long, from plastic bags and bottles to food wrappings and plastic containers. There are also dozens of plastic parts and casings in appliances and gadgets.
Total: about 10 percent by weight (but because they are light, up to 20 percent by volume)

Glass
Glass is very useful, since we can see though it and clean its smooth surfaces thoroughly. But it is also a problem, because it is fragile and breaks easily. Glass is used for bottles, jars, beakers, and cups. It is also used for light bulbs and windows, which occasionally get broken.
Total: about 8 percent

Paper and paper products
These include newspapers, magazines, comics, leaflets, and posters. We also use paper for letters, greeting cards, labels, and for wrapping packages. Cardboard is found in all kinds of packaging and packing. And of course tissues, paper towels, and paper plates are meant to be disposable.
Total: about 30 percent by weight (60 percent by volume)

Chemicals
There are various chemicals in batteries, tablets, and pills and in discarded cleaners, paints, synthetic oils, solvents, weedkillers, and medicines. Many of these have strict safety warnings on their containers. Most households do not produce a great amount of chemical waste, which is more of an industrial problem.
Total: about 3 percent

Clothing and textiles
Some textiles, cloths, and fabrics are made from natural fibers and sources such as wool, cotton, leathers, and rubber. Others are made from artificial fibers, like nylon, rayon, and acrylic.
Total: about 5 percent

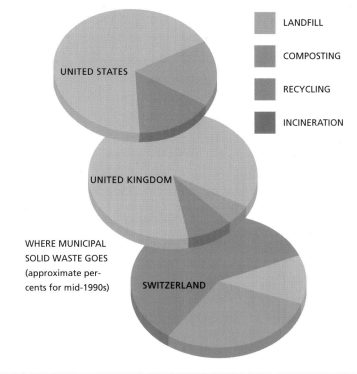

LANDFILL
COMPOSTING
RECYCLING
INCINERATION

UNITED STATES

UNITED KINGDOM

WHERE MUNICIPAL
SOLID WASTE GOES
(approximate per-
cents for mid-1990s)

SWITZERLAND

▲ In a landfill site, waste is dumped, bulldozed, squashed, and covered with layers of soil and more waste. The site may be capped with clay and soil and planted with trees and flowers. But the waste is not gone—it is just hidden.

MUNICIPAL WASTE AND ITS DISPOSAL

Domestic waste is usually collected by garbage trucks and taken to the local waste disposal center. There it is joined by waste from schools, public places like parks, libraries, shopping malls, and picnic areas, and some businesses such as stores, restaurants, theme parks, sports stadiums, concert halls, offices, and small factories. All of this becomes municipal waste. In the United States, one day's municipal waste weighs more than 100 million tons. It would fill 50,000 garbage trucks.

Where does it all go? Most of it is either buried or burned. Other options, now used much less due to pollution problems, include piping waste into waterways, sea dumping, and deep disposal.

BURYING WASTE

In some countries, the bulk of municipal waste goes into landfill—it is tipped into big holes or hollows in the ground. There are more than 5,000 municipal landfill sites in the United States, and more than 60 percent of U.S. municipal waste goes straight into them.

LANDFILL PROBLEMS

Landfill disposal creates many problems. These include smells, windblown garbage and litter, and flies, rats, and other pests that can spread disease. Chemicals, oils, solvents, and toxic metals can dissolve and leak into the groundwater in the soil and rocks, causing pollution. Nutrients and minerals in the wastes may also encourage unwanted blooms of algae and scum.

Organic materials like food scraps rot in the landfill, producing gases—such as methane—that burn well. They may seep thousands of feet through the ground, collect in buildings, and cause explosions. Or they pass into the atmosphere, where they add greatly to the greenhouse effect and global warming.

▲ Fires at garbage dumps and landfill sites are caused by people spilling hot ashes or by inflammable gases such as methane from rotting garbage.

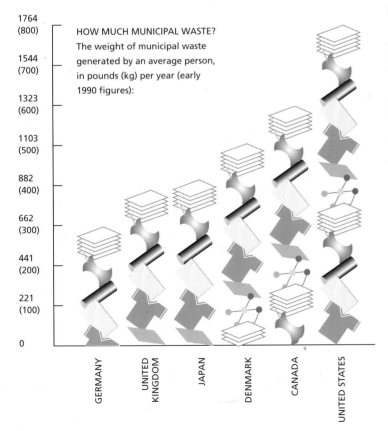

HOW MUCH MUNICIPAL WASTE? The weight of municipal waste generated by an average person, in pounds (kg) per year (early 1990 figures):

1764 (800)
1544 (700)
1323 (600)
1103 (500)
882 (400)
662 (300)
441 (200)
221 (100)
0

GERMANY
UNITED KINGDOM
JAPAN
DENMARK
CANADA
UNITED STATES

BURNING WASTE

Some countries, especially those with small land areas, burn their waste in specialized furnaces called incinerators. The leftover ashes are put into landfill.

Incineration produces smoke, gases, and fumes. Burning mixed wastes can produce harmful chemicals in the smoke. In some countries, laws demand that the fumes are filtered and "scrubbed" to remove these substances. But some environmental campaigners say even the newest filters and scrubbers are not effective enough. No one knows what these hundreds of new chemicals, developed by industry and changed by incineration, may do in years to come.

COMPOSTING

Organic wastes such as paper, cardboard, leftover foods, and garden trimmings may be composted—shredded and put into holes or containers and left to decay. The resulting compost can be recycled as fertilizer. But the organic wastes must be well sorted first. Any trace of toxic substances, such as discarded batteries, can cause dangerous pollution.

INDUSTRIAL WASTE

In developed countries, household waste makes up only about one-twentieth of total waste. Most of the rest comes from industries and businesses such as manufacturing, mining, building, producing energy, agriculture, and transportation. So we could say that industries and businesses of all kinds are responsible for most of the waste mountain.

WASTE AT EVERY STAGE

However "we," the consumers, cannot blame "them," the industries. Every day we buy manufactured items and products—a notepad or a pencil; a can of soda or a bag of chips; a new computer, or a washing machine. Every step on the way from raw material to manufacturer to consumer involves waste. We must take some of the responsibility for the waste.

TYPES OF INDUSTRIAL WASTE

Two major industrial waste makers are agriculture and mining. Farm waste includes fertilizers and pesticides, which get into soil and water and upset the balance of nature. As farm animals are injected or fed with chemicals such as hormones to make them grow faster and resist disease, these chemicals get into the environment, too.

To make the goods and products we consume each year, an average of 10 tons of rocks, stones, and minerals are mined or quarried from the ground, for each person on Earth. This leads to vast open-cast mines that scar the landscape; deep mines that bring problems of subsidence and seepage; huge heaps of waste that can pollute soil and water; and ever-diminishing resources.

▲ Mines and quarries for coal, metals, and minerals such as asbestos (shown here) alter huge areas. The mined rocks contain only small amounts of the product. The rest is waste.

CHEMICAL WASTES

Industry, manufacturing, agriculture, and other businesses use more than 100,000 different chemicals. The list grows by 1,000 each year—almost three every day. Yet no one knows the long-term effects of most of these new chemicals. Where will they be in 50 to 100 years?

BUSINESS FOR PROFIT

Everyone knows that cars cause problems. Making cars produces immense amounts of wastes. Cars produce waste and pollution during their useful lives. And they end up as complex "coffins of waste" containing many different substances that are hard to separate. Around the world, millions of new cars are driven onto the roads every year. Yet automobile manufacturers spend huge sums of money persuading us to buy even more cars.

This shows a major problem in cutting industrial waste. The main aim of big business is not to save waste and help the environment but to make money.

▼ Cars are complex combinations of many different materials that are difficult to sort or recycle.

RADIOACTIVE WASTE

One of the most difficult types of waste to deal with is radioactive waste. It gives off invisible radioactivity that can harm people, animals, plants, and other living things, which will persist for thousands of years. Every day, the world's nuclear industries produce enough radioactive waste to fill between ten and fifteen large trucks. Yet there is no agreement about how or where it should be stored, or how to make it harmless.

SOURCES OF RADIOACTIVE WASTE

Most radioactive waste is from nuclear reactors in power plants that are generating electricity. Some comes from making nuclear weapons. Some also comes from dismantling old nuclear weapons. There are also small nuclear reactors on some ships, submarines, and spacecraft. Research scientists, medical laboratories, and hospitals also use tiny amounts of radioactive materials.

▼ A nuclear power plant's used or spent fuel rods are very dangerous because they still contain some types of fuel. The uranium and plutonium can be removed, purified, and put into new fuel rods, but this "reprocessing" makes yet more radioactive waste.

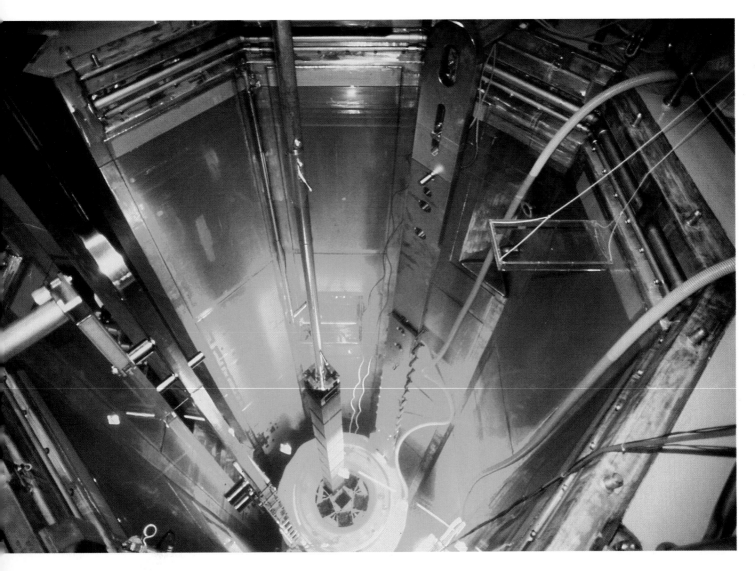

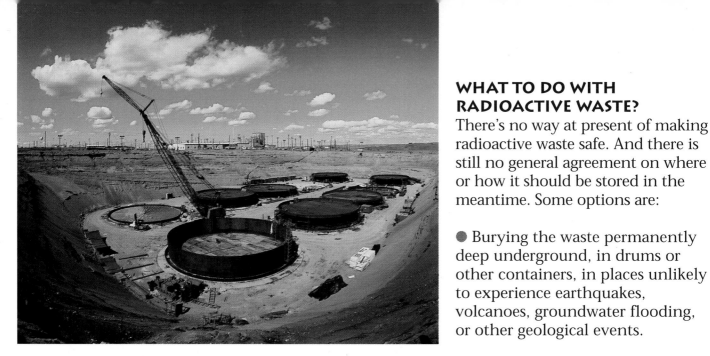

WHAT TO DO WITH RADIOACTIVE WASTE?

There's no way at present of making radioactive waste safe. And there is still no general agreement on where or how it should be stored in the meantime. Some options are:

● Burying the waste permanently deep underground, in drums or other containers, in places unlikely to experience earthquakes, volcanoes, groundwater flooding, or other geological events.

▲ Giant tanks for liquid radioactive waste at the major U.S. nuclear site of Hanford, Washington, hold one million gallons each. They will need monitoring for centuries.

● Burying the waste in the deep seabed. The disposal sites would be far from land and people, preferably in oceanic trenches. Over thousands of years, continental drift would gradually pull the sea floor and the waste deep into the earth. But present international laws prevent such disposal of radioactive waste at sea.

● Shooting the waste into space or at the sun. This would be incredibly expensive, and there's a risk that a rocket might blow up or go off course and crash.

● Nuclear transmutation to change it into a safer form. This means bombarding the waste with more rays and particles. This would use up immense amounts of research, time, and energy.

LEVELS OF RADIOACTIVE WASTE

Radioactive waste is grouped according to the amount of the radiation it gives off, and how long the radiation will last.

● **Low-level** Just above the "safe" level agreed by most nations. The radioactivity lasts for a few decades, then fades to almost normal "background" levels. It can be put in metal drums or other containers and buried, without great hazards.

● **Medium-level** Up to 1,000 times more radioactive than low-level wastes. It needs to be shielded by metal and

concrete. Its radioactivity will last many thousands of years.

● **High-level** The waste has so much radioactive energy that it gets hot. It needs heavy and thick shielding of concrete, metals, and other dense substances. Its radioactivity will last hundreds of thousands, even millions of years. Worldwide, about 33,000 cu. ft. (10,000 cu. m) are produced every year. Much of this is in the United States, which already has stockpiles of 30,000 tons.

▲ Inspectors take samples of suspect waste from a slag pile for laboratory analysis.

TOXIC WASTE

Even in small amounts, toxic substances and wastes are known to harm nature and the environment and damage human health. New chemicals come into use every year, and we have no idea if they will have any long-term toxic effects. Also, industrial accidents continue to happen every few years, producing a huge toll of illness and environmental pollution.

Many toxins do not break down or fade once in the environment. They spread in air and water, get into nature's food chains, and show up in animals as remote as great whales living in the open oceans, polar bears in the Arctic, and seals that live in the Antarctic.

EXPORTING WASTE

"Germany has some of the world's best waste management regulations and some of the world's worst waste export laws. These two factors combine... to enable Germany to keep its home territories clean, at the expense of other regions in the world."
—Andreas Bernsdorff, of Germany's Greenpeace movement

HEAVY METALS

Some of the best-known toxins are so-called heavy metals. They are used in small batteries to power electrical gadgets. But they are very dangerous and cause a long list of health worries when they get into living things, including human bodies.

- Lead—once used in pipes, paints, and fuels such as gasoline—can cause learning difficulties and brain damage. It has been phased out of some fuels, and waste containing lead has to be specially treated in some countries. However in some places, lead is still used to make pipes, bullets, and gunshot.

- Mercury was—and still is, in some places—used in the paper and pulp industries and also in small batteries. It affects the brain and nerves, muscles, the digestive system, and many other body parts.

- Nickel and cadmium are used in NiCad batteries and for coating or plating machine parts. Cadmium is also in solders, alloys, paints and pigments, and TV screens. These metals can harm the lungs and liver.

- Chromium is used for shiny chrome plating, in bearings, and in hard-wearing metal parts. Yet it harms the skin and digestive system.

▲ A doctor checks a young patient for loss of balance—one of the many ill effects caused by the poisonous metal mercury.

OTHER TOXINS

Heavy metals are only part of the toxic waste problem. There are dozens of industrial chemicals that have been found to be toxic, such as:

- Dieldrin, DDT, and other pesticides used in agriculture.
- Some forms of the insulating material asbestos.
- PCBs (polychlorinated biphenyls) useful in electrical goods, lubricants, and printing inks.
- Dioxins made during the manufacture of solvents, preservatives, herbicides, and other substances and also released by burning plastics and other materials.

This list will almost certainly grow. In the future, some of today's supposedly harmless waste chemicals will be discovered to be toxins.

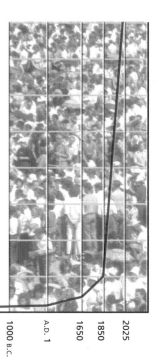

▲ Sewer systems carry all manner of liquid-based materials, from human waste and household effluent to industrial chemicals and vast quantities of storm water.

► The world's population has increased rapidly over the last 150 years, and it is growing at an ever-increasing rate. Standards of living for many people are rising. As this happens, more and more fuel is being used. This in turn is causing more pollution.

World Population (Billions)

8
7
6
5
4
3
2
1

8000 B.C.
1000 B.C.
A.D. 1
1650
1850
2025

HUMAN WASTE

The most numerous large animal on Earth is the human being. There are about 6 billion of us. On average, each person converts a daily intake of foods and drinks into about 5–7 oz. (150–200 g) of solid waste (feces) and 2.6 pt. (1.5 l) of liquid waste (urine). This adds up to an immense amount of waste—human sewage—that will continue to rise as the human population grows.

WASTED WATER

Water is used to flush and carry away most human wastes and chemicals such as soaps, detergents, disinfectants, cleansers, and bleaches from our toilets, sinks, basins, baths, showers, washing machines, dishwashers, and so on. This effluent from daily activities can easily amount to 26 gal. (100 l) per person daily.

This waste may flow along pipes to the sewage treatment works, where it usually mixes with incoming waste water from industry and agriculture. Typically, solids and clear water are separated during treatment to leave sewage sludge, a mixture of sewage and wastes from hundreds of sources, containing thousands of chemicals.

WATERBORNE DISEASES

Since ancient times, infectious diseases such as cholera, typhoid, and dysentery have spread by water contaminated with sewage from sufferers. Weil's disease, ear infections, and digestive upsets are spread in a similar way. Safe treatment of waste sewage and effluent reduces illness and suffering —and this saves on the medical costs of caring for the sick.

▼ Raw sewage pours into a bay near Rio de Janeiro, Brazil, causing a major pollution incident. There are risks of disease as well as harm to wildlife and damage to fish catches.

BACK TO THE LAND?

An obvious use for sewage sludge is to spread it on the land as fertilizer. But there are problems of smells and spreading waterborne diseases (see box). The many chemicals, especially from industrial waste water, could also cause great problems of contamination and pollution.

VARIATIONS ON SEWAGE DISPOSAL

Most developed countries have laws saying that sewage and effluent must be treated before disposal. But in some places, human sewage and effluent go untreated into rivers, lakes, and the sea. In areas with few people, the wastes may be recycled naturally by plants and animals. But where people crowd together, especially at tourist resorts, there is often so much sewage that it cannot be recycled. It may float in shallow water and wash up on the beach, along with flushed-away items like diapers, toilet paper, medical pills, needles, and syringes.

WAR ON WASTE

It is obvious that we cannot go on producing huge amounts of waste. We are using up our planet's precious materials and resources, which will run out sooner rather than later; we are filling landfill sites with mountains of garbage; and we are polluting the soil, water, and air with substances from waste, some of which are very toxic. We must act quickly. Some people and countries have already begun with increasingly effective campaigns and systems to tackle the waste problem.

▲ Mixed solid waste is too difficult, costly, and hazardous to sort and recycle. Sorting at the source is a major step in the recycling effort.

NO WASTE AT ALL?

Will there always be waste, no matter how hard we try? Many environmental campaigners say "no." They believe that by accepting that some raw materials, energy, and other resources will always go to waste, we are accepting defeat. There are various catchy ideas and phrases intended to focus people's attention on the problem, including:

- **Zero Waste** We should not give in before we start. Our aim should be to leave no waste at all.
- **The Four Rs** Reduce, recycle, re-use, reprocess. We should aim to cut the amounts of waste we produce, and then recycle, re-use, and reprocess any that are left over.

DON'T MIX IT!

One of the major problems in dealing with wastes is that they are often mixed up. Many different types of waste, such as tin cans, glass bottles, cardboard, and vegetable peelings, end up in the same plastic bag too often. This makes them difficult to sort, re-use, or recycle. Collecting different types of wastes separately, or sorting them cheaply and effectively, is a key feature in dealing with waste.

FINDING THE BALANCE

Other environmental campaigners recognize that there will always be waste. Their main aims are to minimize its production and to find uses for any wastes that are produced.

We can all help, but big companies and governments will have the greatest effect. By changing their attitudes and using new technologies, new systems, and passing new laws and regulations, companies and governments can turn waste reduction, collection, recycling, and disposal into a big, profitable and—most important —sustainable business.

A CHANGE IN LIFESTYLES

The war on waste involves changing our attitudes, expectations, and ways of living. We should get used to the idea that minimizing waste is essential for our environment, our future, and the whole world. This will certainly involve people in rich, industrial countries making some reductions and sacrifices in their luxurious, comfortable lifestyles.

▼ Scavenging at garbage dumps is very dangerous, with risks of cuts, injuries, disease, and poisonous gases. But some people are so poor that they have little choice.

BETTER WASTE DISPOSAL

▼ This fish has two cancers growing on its side. They are probably the result of industrial waste being pumped into the sea.

Waste can go in one of three directions—up (into the atmosphere after incineration), down (into landfill sites, lakes, and seas), or around (that is, recycled). The two main methods of waste disposal—landfill and incineration—were described on pages 10 and 11. New ideas and technologies can make these much safer and more effective, cutting the costs in terms of finance, risks to the environment, and hazards to human health. Of course, they should be carried out alongside the aims of cutting waste production at its source and increasing re-use and recycling of waste.

LESS LEAKY LANDFILLS

Landfills can be improved by choosing better locations. These are checked in terms of topography (the shape of the landscape), the types of soil and rocks below ground, and the movement of rainwater at the surface and the groundwater underneath. This helps cut down on the leakage of water and dissolved chemicals—called the "leachate."

A landfill can be lined with clay or a plastic sheet to help keep in any water and dissolved chemicals, which drain and settle in the lowest area. The leachate is then drawn off through pipes and stored in a nearby tank for safe disposal.

Explosive methane buildup can be reduced by collecting the gases through pipes in the landfill. The methane can then be burned off safely—or, in a big site, burned as fuel in a power plant to generate electricity. A large landfill can produce enough methane to make electricity for 10,000 homes.

◀ Instead of causing explosions or adding to the greenhouse effect, methane from landfill sites can be collected by pipes to fuel generators and make useful electricity.

"Waste police" are usually government agents or inspectors who monitor the business of waste management and disposal. Their job is to keep a check on the people who collect and dispose of waste and to make sure they have the correct permits and licenses.

Some unscrupulous dealers advertise themselves as waste experts, charge a fee to collect specialist wastes—such as toxic chemicals from a factory—and then simply dump the chemicals in the countryside, with no proper precautions.

▲ This combined refuse plant and power station at Newcastle, England, sorts garbage, removes metals for recycling, dries, and compresses the remains into RDF (refuse-derived fuel) pellets, and burns them to generate 2.5 megawatts of electricity plus heating for 1,700 homes and buildings.

IMPROVED INCINERATION

Some incinerators do not just burn waste: they use the heat that is released by burning to drive generators and produce electricity. This system could be extended to all new incinerators and also improved further.

In a normal incinerator, only about half the energy in the waste (given off as heat) is turned into electricity. But the remaining heat can be used to drive industrial processes or heat buildings. This puts more than 65 percent of the energy in the waste to worthwhile use.

It is possible to get even more heat from the waste by carefully controlling the temperature at which it burns and for how long. Doing this also produces less fumes, toxic vapors, and ash.

Due to problems of incineration on land, some countries used incinerator ships. The fumes were produced far out at sea, and the ash was dumped there. But this has caused many pollution problems. The United States stopped ocean incineration in 1982, and it was stopped in Europe in 1994.

BE A WASTE WATCHER

Each week the average household in a developed country goes through 4 glass bottles or jars, 13 cans, 3 plastic bottles, and 11 lbs. (5 kg) of paper. Surveys show that nine people out of ten think that waste watching and recycling are important. Yet six people out of ten still dump these items straight into the trash.

Waste watching, like recycling, can begin at home. As we change our household habits and domestic attitudes, we can also spread the message into communities, schools, businesses, and other organizations. The central messages are:

- Make sure any process or item is produced in the least wasteful way, creating less waste in the first place.
- Rather than throwing it away, re-use it or recycle it yourself.
- If you can't, persuade others to do so, or make sure it goes into a proper recycling plan.

▼ Bags of presorted domestic waste, as here in Germany, can be recycled quickly and effectively, saving time, money, and resources.

AT THE STORES

We can make a great impact on reducing waste, by changing the way we shop. This makes less waste in our daily lives, and it also shows manufacturers that their low-waste products are more popular. For example:

- For any nonessential item—do you really need it? Think for a while. No purchase means no waste at all.
- Does it have to be new? Many items, like famous books or old-fashioned clothing and hats, can be bought secondhand from all kinds of sources.
- Avoid products with excessive packaging.
- Buy products for which you can get refills (for example, many detergents).
- Avoid disposable items, even if the nondisposable versions take a little time to clean or re-equip for re-use.
- Choose products made from recycled materials.
- Choose products made in environmentally friendly ways.
- Choose long-life products: they may cost more but in the long term usually represent better value and less waste.
- Take your old shopping bags back to the store so that you do not need new ones, or take another bag to use.
- Buy in bulk if possible, which reduces waste of all kinds, especially containers and packaging.
- Buy local products if possible, since they involve less waste from long-distance transportation.

▶ Unlike canned, frozen, or prepared foods, fresh fruit and vegetables are often sold with little or no packaging.

WASTE WATCHING AT HOME

First and foremost, sort and save as much waste as possible, for recycling. Keep different containers for drink cans, food cans, organic matter, paper, metals, plastic bottles, and other recyclable items (see page 36). Also:

- Discuss waste watching with your family and friends. Have they got any good tips you can share?
- If you have a backyard, start a compost pile.
- Try to mend or repair things rather than throw them away. Think of the time you spend doing this as "earning" the money you would have to pay for a new item.
- Spend a few minutes checking that household detergents, cleaners, and other chemicals are low-waste and environmentally friendly.
- Use paper where possible, rather than plastic. It can usually be recycled more easily.
- Around the house, have proper insulation, cook in bulk, turn off unnecessary lights, and use low-energy and long-life light bulbs, machines, and appliances.
- Save heat, electricity, and other forms of energy, as well as water. This cuts down waste during its production and also cuts down on household bills.

▼ A compost pile helps to recycle "green wastes" from nature—such as grass cuttings, vegetable peelings, and food scraps—back into the soil.

IN THE COMMUNITY

Help others realize the size of the waste problem and do something about it, without becoming a pest or pain in the neck. Gentle methods include discussion, education, and persuasion. Stronger methods include advertising, demonstrations, and petitions.

- Litter is waste and also unsightly. It is a danger to wildlife. Animals get trapped in cans, bottles, plastic string, and ties, swallow bright objects, or get cut on sharp edges. Encourage people to make less litter and to take it home for recycling.

- If local trash cans are emptied too rarely, or are even absent, inform the sanitation department.
- Report any illegal dumping or pollution promptly to the local sanitation department.
- Ask if local schools, offices, and factories have policies on saving waste and recycling. A box for waste paper, to be recycled, is a simple start.
- Write to local power plants, incinerators, and industries about their waste-saving and recycling policies. Do they try to buy low-waste and recycled products? Try to get an answer.
- Join or start a waste-watch group or club.

▼ This illegal garbage dump could hide toxic substances, such as mercury from batteries or lighting tubes.

▼ Litter and nature do not mix. Animals suffer distress, pain, and injury from waste thrown away by thoughtless people.

27

Governments can help to combat waste by passing laws that force industries to create less of it. They can also use taxes to punish wastefulness and encourage more careful use of resources, recycling, and re-use.

The 1992 Earth Summit in Rio de Janeiro—which was attended by the leaders of many countries from around the world—suggested shifting taxation from people and work to resources and pollution. This means people would pay tax money to their government, mainly according to how much of the world's resources and raw materials they used up, and how much waste and pollution they produced, rather than mainly on how much money they earned.

WHAT INDUSTRY CAN DO

Most of the waste in our world is produced by industries such as mining, quarrying, metal production, manufacturing, construction, and intensive farming. Industries and big business have central roles to play in reducing waste. Many are already doing so.

STARTING AT THE END?

The war on industrial waste has many battlefields. One is the debate about "end-of-pipe" technologies. This refers to reducing the harmful effects of waste by adding filters, screening, scrubbers, and other machinery to factory outfall pipes, chimneys, and garbage cans. These remove some of the toxins and pollutants. But the extra technology costs extra money and produces its own wastes. And it does little to reduce waste creation in the first place. What is really needed are "clean technologies," where minimal waste and maximum recycling are built in from the start, at the design stage, not added on at the end. They may be expensive to research and set up, but the long-term benefits are great savings on energy and raw materials and increased recycling and re-use.

▶ Filter systems, such as this sludge filter for waste water, need constant monitoring and maintenance. It is far better to reduce the amount of waste at the source.

● Plastics are increasing in cars, to save weight and to reduce corrosion. Some plastic parts, such as bumpers, dashboards, and door linings, are already recycled. Usually they are turned into more bumpers.

● About half of a new car is sheet steel in the bodywork. Nine-tenths could be recycled, provided the parts are easily separated and sorted.

● Oil filters, gasoline filters, and similar parts could be squeezed to release their fluid, then compressed into bricks for furnace fuel.

● Fluids such as oil, gasoline, brake fluid, and radiator anti-freeze could be drained off and re-used or treated for recycling.

● Batteries enter a well-established recycling system, in nations such as the United States, where more than nine-tenths of all car batteries are disposed of carefully and recycled.

● Tires can be recycled in several ways. In the United States, 20 percent are made into re-tread tires for further use, 15 percent are incinerated to yield heat energy, and 10 percent are shredded and granulated for rubberized surfaces on athletic fields, parking lots, and public spaces.

A FEW SIMPLE STEPS FOR INDUSTRIES

● Make parts more easy to recycle by making them of one substance, not combining metals, plastics, and other materials in one component.

● Standardize metals and alloys in cans and containers, so they are easier to recycle.

● Standardize bottle shapes and sizes so they can be re-used in the filling machines.

● Appoint a person responsible for reducing waste and increasing recycling.

● Introduce targets for reducing spills and leaks.

● Keep different types of wastes separate, for reprocessing and recycling.

● Accept the "precautionary principle" that wastes must be proved safe by their maker, rather than proved harmful by other people. And accept that polluters have to pay for the cleanup.

▲ Cars and other road vehicles are a gigantic industry around the globe—and still a gigantic source of waste. Governments in the United States, Germany, and other nations, and major carmakers such as General Motors, Ford, Volkswagen, and BMW, are devising plans to make cars more recyclable. By the year 2015, some major manufacturers aim to leave only 5 percent of a car (by weight) for landfill disposal.

RE-USE AND RECYCLE

W aste does not have to be wasted. It can have many uses, especially if it can be recycled or re-used.

RE-USE

Re-use means using the same item again—and perhaps again and again. It may need to be repaired every so often, as with second-hand clothes and toys, but it can last a long time. Re-use has been carried out for centuries in the form of clothes, toys, cutlery, crockery, and heirlooms handed down from one generation to the next. Secondhand shops and antique dealers rely on re-use. In the huge garbage dumps of some cities, people make a living by sorting and picking through the waste and re-using or selling what they can.

▼ In some areas, times are set aside for people to pick through a garbage dump and re-use and recycle what they can. But it is a hazardous process.

RECYCLING

Recycling mainly involves processing materials so that they can be used as raw materials for another industry. They may end up in much the same product, such as cardboard boxes recycled into yet more cardboard boxes. Or they may be very different, as when iron and steel from cans and cars are re-smelted to form scaffolding poles or reinforcing bars in concrete. The scrap metal business has a long history of recycling iron-based metals, while aluminum recycling has grown up mainly in the last 20 years.

SORTING IT OUT

The major problem with recycling general domestic and municipal waste is that it is so mixed. A black plastic bag of garbage could contain all kinds of substances and items. These different types of wastes can be sorted at modern recycling centers, but this costs time, machinery, and money. Sorting garbage into clear plastic bags so that glass, metals, paper, plastic, and so on are easily identified is much more efficient.

Sorting can be done in three main ways:

- **Bring**, where people bring materials to specialized sites like recycling centers.
- **Collect at Curbside**, where household wastes are left ready-sorted for collection by local authorities or specialized groups.
- **Centralized**, where mixed waste is sorted at a recycling center. For example, ferrous (iron and steel) items for scrap metal can be recovered from general waste, using a powerful magnet.

POWERED BY WASTE

Materials do not have to be recycled or re-used in a physical sense. Biodegradable waste such as straw, paper, animal manure, and food leftovers can be composted or rotted commercially in huge "digesters," to make gases such as methane. This can be burned for heating in homes, factories and industrial processes or burned as fuel in power stations to generate electricity, thereby saving fossil fuels. The remaining ashes and compost are then recycled as fertilizer on the land.

IT CAN BE DONE!

In the European nations' household waste league, 1995, Germany was one of the leaders in terms of the amounts of wastes it recycled. It achieved this success relatively quickly, as shown in the graph below. This has cost a lot in time, money, publicity, and setting up recycling plans, but it shows what can be done.

▲ Clearly labeled containers make it easy to sort and save wastes in the home and to gather them in commercial quantities for collection.

▶ These graphs show how Germany increased the amount of waste that it recycles. The bars indicate the percentage of each type of waste that was recycled in 1992 and in 1995.

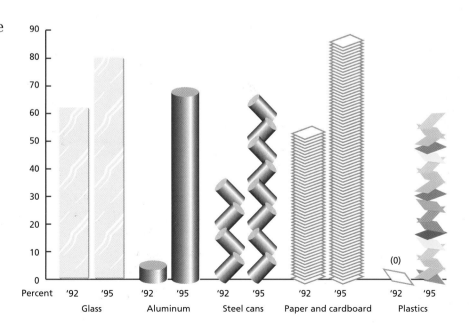

Percent	'92	'95	'92	'95	'92	'95	'92	'95	'92	'95
	Glass		Aluminum		Steel cans		Paper and cardboard		Plastics	

▲ Plastics were once seen as "villains"—pure waste, impossible to recycle. Now they can be viewed as a valuable resource for PCR (postconsumer recycling).

BENEFITS AND DRAWBACKS

Is it really worth making a special round-trip in the car just to take one glass jar to the nearest recycling center? Most people would say "no." The gain from recycling one jar would be far less than the car's use of fuel, the air pollution, general wear and tear, and many other drawbacks. This comparison of benefits and drawbacks applies to many aspects of re-use and recycling.

PARTS OF THE WHOLE

Some of the results of comparing pros and cons are surprising. For instance, compared with traditional glass bottles, many people see plastic bottles as bad, using up valuable raw materials in their production. But a plastic bottle uses less than half the energy to make and transport and consumes less than one-twentieth of the weight of raw materials of an equivalent glass bottle. It also needs only one-third as much water and generates less than half the total waste. Changing from glass bottles and other glass containers to plastic ones can save about $1,000 per year for an average passenger jet plane. Because the plastic is much lighter, the plane needs less fuel.

THE BATTLE OF THE BAGS

A scientific study looked at the resources and materials needed to make one plastic bag and one paper bag of similar size and strength. Compared with the paper version, the plastic bag:

- Used about half as much energy in its overall manufacture.
- Caused half as much atmospheric pollution (gases and particles in the air).
- Required 100 times less water.
- Is recycled much more easily, compared with 10 years ago.

So the assumption that plastics are wasteful, while paper is not, is difficult to support. But this is only true for today. About one-thirtieth of petroleum oil is made into plastic products. One day, the oil may run out. Trees used to make paper can continue to be grown, so they should never run out.

WHERE DO WE STOP?

Such comparisons can become very complicated. For example:

- A low-energy, fluorescent long-life light bulb costs perhaps 20 times more to buy than a standard incandescent (filament) bulb.

- But it consumes far less electricity, so over its full long-life, the total purchase and running costs are half as much as the standard bulb.

- However, the long-life bulb contains mercury, which is a costly raw material and a dangerous pollutant.

- Yet, more mercury is released in generating the extra electricity for the standard bulb, compared with the long-life one.

- And, if the long-life bulb is disposed of properly, its mercury can be recovered for re-use.

- Even so, standard bulbs are far cheaper, less complex, and less wasteful to manufacture at the factory, compared with long-life ones.

So the equation continues, swinging this way and that and never reaching the end.

▲ Long-life, low-wattage light bulbs cost more to manufacture and buy than these cheap, mass-produced versions. But they use less electricity and last longer.

RECYCLING BEGINS AT HOME

Before you throw anything away, make sure that it really is waste, of no use to anyone. If it can't be re-used, can it be recycled? If the answer is "yes," you will need to sort it first and then take it to your nearest recyling center. Here are some ideas:

▲ A tiny amount of thought, organization, and effort can lead to huge benefits for recycling. Group projects, with neighbors and friends, or colleagues at school or work, are especially effective.

● **Paper, cardboard, and board** Put old newspapers, bits of cardboard and card-based packaging in one pile and glossy magazines and other glossy paper in another. Fold or crush boxes flat, to save space. As with all recycling, check the list on the recycling container so that you do not put in unsuitable items.

● **Food cans** These are usually steel (tinplate or steel plated with tin). Test them with a magnet—it attracts steel and iron-based items. Rinse them first, to reduce smell, flies, and general contamination. Be careful of sharp edges on lids or pulltabs. Crush the cans underfoot or with a crusher to save space.

● **Drink cans** In many places, you will pay a 5-cent deposit when you buy a soft drink can. In these states, when you return these cans you may claim a rebate. In some states, however, this law does not apply. Before you return the cans, be sure to clean them thoroughly. You will have to dispose of other aluminum products separately, according to your community's rules.

MAKING SACRIFICES

"The real answer to environmental problems is not just recycling but leading simpler lifestyles, generating less waste, treating things with care, not being slaves to fashion, and learning to shoulder responsibility and make sacrifices."
—Ken Morishita, leading Japanese eco-management consultant

◀ Clothes and textiles from the recycling container are sorted quickly and efficiently. However, unsuitable items like oil-soaked rags can ruin an entire batch.

● **Glass** Glass bottles, jars, and other containers should also be rinsed carefully and then put in containers for glass. Some recycling centers take only one color of glass per container.

● **Plastic** The systems and technologies for recycling plastic products are gradually improving. Plastic bags and PET-plastic bottles are now collected at many recycling centers, especially at supermarkets.

● **Clothes and textiles** Clothes, sheets, blankets, rags, and other textiles can go into the textile bank. Check the list on the container there so you do not put in unsuitable items. Some centers also collect shoes.

● **Organic waste** Waste or out-of-date foods, meal leftovers, peelings, and kitchen scraps make excellent food for worms and other items in a compost pile.

▼ Larger numbers and bigger quantities from group recycling, as here in Colombia, help save extra time and money—and even generate income for the group.

COMMUNITY RECYCLING

In many ways, groups of people can do more than separate individuals. Numbers of people can campaign, exert pressure, raise petitions, and cause change. Groups can be formed at playgroups and nursery schools, in a village or street or neighborhood, at clubs for sports or hobbies, at work, and by people of all ages—children, adults, families, and the retired.

RECYCLING GLASS

Glass makes up one of the largest groups of recycled materials. As with other types of recycling, the first stage in the process is to persuade enough people to collect enough items to make recycling and reprocessing realistic and cost-effective. Then, the materials produced after recycling must have a market—people who want to buy them.

People in the United Kingdom use six billion glass jars and bottles yearly. About 27 percent of household waste glass, mainly bottles and jars, gets to recycling centers. There is one center per 2,800 people. In the Netherlands, the glass recycling rate is over 65 percent, and there is one recycling center per 1,200 inhabitants.

The recycling process is relatively simple. The glass is cleaned, crushed, heated, melted, and added to varying proportions of new molten glass and blown or pressed into new items. This recycling can happen again and again.

Recycled glass saves up to 25 percent of the energy costs compared with making new glass. This cuts fuel use and air pollution. It also saves on raw materials, mainly silica sand, limestone, and soda minerals.

▲ Recycling most substances, such as glass, relies on having plenty of material. Greater quantities mean greater savings.

▼ Cleaned and crushed glass chippings are checked for quality and color, before being fed into the furnace and melted down for new bottles, jars, and containers.

HOW TO HELP GLASS RECYCLING

- Put the correct colors of glass into the different containers at the recycling site. Mixing them causes problems and makes the process less efficient.

- If bottles are refillable or returnable, refill or return them instead of putting them in the recycling bin. They are usually thicker and stronger than nonreturnable ones, with twice the weight of glass, to withstand repeated cleaning, filling, and sealing. So recycling them too early wastes this extra glass.

- Expect and accept glass items that are made of recycled glass. It may not be quite so smooth and transparent.

▼ Young people are often most enthusiastic about recycling and re-use. They see that it will help safeguard their own future.

RECYCLING PAPER PRODUCTS

In theory, over 90 percent of paper products could be recycled. But around the world, the actual figure is less than 30 percent. Most paper, cardboard, and board products are made from the squashed, matted, dried fibers of cellulose, which came originally from wood.

In recycling, the paper and cardboard are shredded, mixed with water, and beaten by blades into a mush. This is whirled around in a big drum. Heavy pieces such as staples, clips, and other metal items sink to the bottom. Light inks, coatings, and other chemicals float to the top. The middle section of soggy fibers is screened and filtered and becomes pulp—raw material for the paper-making process.

Paper making consumes vast amounts of wood, chemicals, water, and energy. Making recycled paper can save between one-third and two-thirds of the energy compared with new paper. But this recycling is also a complex process. Waste-paper merchants may sort their collections into ten or more groups, according to the type and quality of the paper.

▲ This corrugated cardboard may be heading for its fourth trip through the recycling system, having previously been high-quality writing paper, recycled notepads, and newspaper.

DOES RECYCLED PAPER SAVE TREES?

Not necessarily, although it certainly reduces the number of trees we use.

● The tiny cellulose fibers gradually shorten and fray during each pass through the recycling process. As a result, more trees are always required to produce fresh fibers for quality paper products.

● Paper recycling could never reach 100 percent, as it does for aluminum. Besides the problem of fiber deterioration, some paper goes into storage, for written records and books. Also some is burned, contaminated, or rotted back into the soil.

● In most countries, paper is made from softwood trees that are grown as a crop, just like growing wheat or potatoes on a farm. This is designed to be a sustainable process. It is not part of the unsustainable use of hardwoods, which is affecting the world's tropical forests.

HOW TO HELP PAPER RECYCLING

- Remove staples, paper clips, and other nonpaper items before recycling.
- Follow the instructions on the recycling container, and put in only the advised types of paper.
- Buy recycled paper products, including computer printout paper, package wrapping, envelopes, and toilet paper. Some types of corrugated cardboard, for packages and boxes, are almost 100 percent recycled paper.
- Find out about other uses for waste paper, such as shredded mulch for compost, loft insulation, fiberboard, molded cardboard, and animal bedding.

▲ At this Danish paper mill, 100 trucks arrive daily with bales of waste paper and board. These are sorted and graded so that they can be recycled to best advantage.

▲ Metal recycling is a heavy-duty process. Large sheets are cut with torches, and the heavy scrap is dumped by big cranes into powerful crushers and shredders.

RECYCLING METALS

Iron and aluminum are numbers one and two in the list of the world's most-used metals. Iron is the main metal in steel, and steel is the most-used metal in construction, engineering, and vehicle manufacture. The scrap iron and steel business has been around for centuries. Aluminum production is a much newer mass industry. But purifying this metal from raw materials is so costly that aluminum recycling has quickly become established in the past 20 years.

FERROUS METALS—IRON AND STEEL

Scrap metal is sorted with machinery such as giant electro-magnets, which attract iron and other ferrous metals. Copper, brass, lead, aluminum, and other nonferrous metals are processed separately. The iron or steel is turned into a vast range of products, including garbage cans, fencing, and more cans.

Worldwide, more than half of all steel is made from recycled scrap. Making iron and steel from suitable scrap metal saves about 75 percent of the energy, enormous amounts of leftover mine spoil, and huge quantities of water used to make the steel in the first place.

SOURCES OF SCRAP METAL

● Large industries that use iron and steel as raw materials, such as vehicle manufacturers, machine makers, metalworkers, and producers of nails, screws, and fittings.
● Demolition of buildings and dismantling metal equipment like construction vehicles.
● "Junk" metal from old fridges, washing machines, bicycles, tools, and other domestic objects.

ALUMINUM

In theory, aluminium can be recycled almost 100 percent. This saves more than 90 percent of energy costs. It also saves tropical forest areas, which is where the main aluminum ore, bauxite, is mined.

In the United States, aluminum can recycling began in 1976. Now, over 70 percent of cans there are recycled—one of the highest rates in the world. The Swedish rate is over 90 percent.

▲ Mining bauxite—the main source of aluminum—means removing the entire surface covering. Even with replanting, it takes many years for the natural habitat to regenerate.

NEW CONVERTERS FROM OLD

Vehicle catalytic converters were developed to remove harmful substances from exhaust fumes. Catalytic converters have brought new problems about how to deal with the rare metals platinum, rhodium, and palladium inside them. Instead of discarding these rare and possibly harmful metals, a new recycling business is growing up around them. The metals can be recovered and refined for re-use in converters for other industrial uses, at a rate of 70 percent for platinum and 90 percent for rhodium. The United States has a well-developed network of agents who collect catalytic converters. The system is also growing in Europe.

▶ U.S. factories produce 300 million aluminum cans daily. More than two-thirds are recycled.

RECYCLING PLASTICS

Paper, iron, and glass have been recycled for many years. But plastics are a recent invention: about 50 years ago, there were hardly any. So plastic recycling technology is at an early stage.

There are many different kinds of plastics, and each has to be recycled in a different way; some cannot be recycled at all. New technology for shredding and sorting the different types uses X rays, infrared beams, electrostatic attraction, flotation tanks, and additive chemicals to identify different plastics.

WHAT DOES RECYCLED PLASTIC MAKE?

Many areas now have plastic bottle and plastic bag recycling centers. PET is the most important plastic for recycling. It is used to make more PET bottles, vehicle parts, and casings on electrical machines or spun into fiber stuffings for pillows, furniture, and insulated clothes.

There are many growing uses for recycled PET and other plastics. They include bags, sacks, park benches, roofing and wall sheets, bricks, tiles, pipes, road and industrial surfaces, road cones, fencing, garden furniture, seed trays, cases for cassettes and CDs—and, more recently, PCR (post consumer recycled) textiles and clothing with fleecy fibers resembling polyester or acrylic.

▼ Fence posts made from recycled plastic last longer than wood, reduce the amounts of plastic going into landfill, and are cheaper to make than metal ones.

RECYCLING OFFICE, ELECTRONIC, AND TECHNICAL WASTES

Televisions, videos, computers, printers, fax machines, monitor screens, photocopiers, telephones, hi-fi systems, and other electronic machinery are advancing at a tremendous rate. This produces mountains of old, out-of-date "gray goods." What can be done with them?

● The whole device if still working could go to another user.

● Cartridges and containers for toners and inks can be refilled to be used again in photocopiers and printers.

● Valuable materials in the electrical circuits—such as gold, silver, and copper—can sometimes be recovered. So can plastic parts and cases and some of the circuits.

● Basic electrical parts such as batteries and transformers may be recyclable.

Offices, schools, and similar places should enquire if waste collectors and disposers have plans to recycle electronic equipment and "gray goods." The more machines, the more cost effective this is.

▶ Even though the mass production of computers began only in the 1970s, very few are designed for recycling. Instead, old computers are normally thrown away.

BIODEGRADABLE PLASTICS

There are various kinds of plastics that naturally degrade or rot. Some are "eaten" by bacteria, fungi, and other microbes; others break down in sunlight. These plastics cannot be recycled in the usual way since they would "contaminate" further plastic items and make them weak and fragile. Also biodegrading means that some of the resources and energy used to make the plastic are lost. After some early success, the future for biodegradable plastics looks uncertain.

THE FUTURE

Waste has been a problem for thousands of years. Because of its ever-increasing quantities, the problem is now becoming a crisis. But there is increasing hope, too. More people are becoming aware of the need to reduce our creation of waste drastically. Waste management and disposal are governed by ever stricter regulations. Re-use and recycling are becoming big business. Manufacturers and industries are taking notice of pressure from campaign groups and the general public.

▼ Fast-developing nations also have fast-growing waste.

▲ Televisions have been around for about half a century, but only now are people starting to recycle old televisions.

THE INTERNATIONAL DIMENSION

These hopeful signs are seen mainly in the rich, industrialized countries. Globally, the majority of the waste mountain will soon be produced in the fast-developing regions such as southern and Southeast Asia and South America.

THE HOPES

If the developing nations increase their consumption of important resources—such as petroleum, copper, cobalt, and nickel—to those of the United States in the mid-1990s, then the supplies of all these resources will have run out by about 2020. It is easy for rich nations to point at this fact and to tell others not to increase their consumptions. But people in developing countries might well respond—why? The rich countries already have comfortable but high-waste lifestyles. Why shouldn't others? And if using up resources and producing wastes are great problems, why don't rich countries, who are responsible for much of it, stop doing it?

CHANGES AND SACRIFICES

It is impossible for everyone in the world to have the comfortable, convenient lifestyle now enjoyed by people in rich countries. It is also impossible for people in rich countries to go on enjoying this lifestyle. It is far too extravagant in terms of wasting materials, resources, and energy. We cannot go on buying endless new products while throwing away old ones. We must realize that new can be bad, while old can be good.

This will involve changes and sacrifices for millions of richer people in more prosperous countries. It will probably mean slightly less comfort, choice, and convenience. But it will have to happen—sometime and somehow.

GLOSSARY

BIODEGRADABLE Able to degrade—through decay and rot—naturally the action of the weather and living things.

EFFLUENT Waste water and other substances from a waste pipe (outfall), which could be from a house, factory, or treatment plant.

EMISSIONS Waste gases and solids discharged into the atmosphere from chimneys and vehicle exhausts.

GLOBAL WARMING The gradual warming up of the surface of the planet as a result of a change in the composition of atmospheric gases, especially an increase in the percentages of carbon dioxide from burning and methane from biodegrading.

GREENHOUSE GAS A gas that helps trap warmth in the atmosphere and thus contributes to global warming.

HEAVY METALS Certain metals such as mercury, cadmium, platinum, lead, and gold, which are heavy in weight, and which are purified for specialized uses in industry. But even in tiny amounts they are poisonous to plants, animals, and people, and they are not biodegradable.

INCINERATION Burning, usually at a high and controlled temperature.

METHANE A naturally occurring gas, both in the fossil-fuel gas fields found deep in the ground, and as a product of decay when living matter rots or biodegrades.

ORGANIC Part of, or a product of, or made from, a living thing.

PCR Postconsumer recycling—that is, recycling after an item has actually been used and is destined for waste—contrast with reprocessing.

PET Polyethylene terephthalate; a type of plastic from which drink bottles are often made.

PVC Polyvinylchloride; a plastic often used for blister packs, food trays, and non-carbonated soft-drink bottles.

RADIATION Energy in the form of invisible rays and particles given off by radioactive substances such as uranium.

RECYCLED MATERIAL Substances that are made by recycling from potential waste.

RECYCLING Processing items and materials that would otherwise be disposed of as waste, so they can be used again as raw materials.

REPROCESSING Recovering industrial trimmings, offcuts, and spare scrap, which have not reached the stage of a consumer item. Contrast this with PCR.

RE-USE Using the same item or object over and over again, perhaps with maintenance and repairs along the way, but no large-scale changes.

SUSTAINABLE A way of using resources that does not threaten their long-term survival or the survival of the plants and animals, including humans, that depend on them.

WASTE WATER Water after it has been used by people or industry, and which must be treated (made cleaner) before it can be allowed back into rivers or the sea.

FURTHER INFORMATION

BOOKS TO READ

Blashfield, Jean F. & Wallace B. Black. *Recycling* (Saving Planet Earth). Danbury, CT: Children's Press, 1991.

Coote, Roger, ed. *Atlas of the Environment.* Austin, TX: Raintree Steck-Vaughn, 1992.

Elkington, John, et. al. *Going Green: A Kid's Handbook to Saving the Planet.* New York: Puffin Books, 1990.

Gardner, Robert. *Working Together Against the Destruction of the Environment* (Library of Social Activism). New York: The Rosen Group, 1994.

Gay, Kathlyn. *Caretakers of the Earth* (Better Earth). Springfield, NJ: Enslow Publications, 1993.

Gutnik, Martin J. *Experiments That Explore Recycling.* Brookfield, CT: Millbrook Press, 1992.

——. *Recycling: Learning the Four R's: Reduce, Reuse, Recycle, Recover* (Better Earth) Springfield, NJ: Enslow Publications, 1993.

Langone, John. *Our Endangered Earth: Our Environment and What We Can Do to Save It.* Boston: Little Brown, 1992.

McVey, Vicki. *The Sierra Club Kid's Guide to Planet Care and Repair.* San Francisco: Sierra Club, 1993.

ADDRESSES TO WRITE TO

National Association of Chemical Recyclers
1200 G Street, Suite 800
Washington, D.C. 20005

National Recycling Coalition
1727 King Street, Suite 105
Alexandria, VA 22314

New York State Association for Reduction, Reuse and Recycling, Inc.
51 Fulton Street
Poughkeepsie, NY 12601

International Solid Waste Association
Bremerholm 1
Copenhagen
Denmark DK-1069

Association of Post-Consumer Plastic Recyclers
1275 K Street N.W., #501
Washington, D.C. 20005

Canadian Association of Recycling Industries
50 Gervais Drive #502
Don Mills, ON
Canada M3C 1Z3

Vehicle Recycling Partnership
12000 Oakland Avenue, M.C. 418-4100
Highland Park, MI 48288-1001

E-MAIL AND WORLD WIDE WEB SITES

http://www.recycle.net/recycle/Associations/
Provides a list of agencies and organizations that deal with all types of recycling.

http://www.newscientist.com
The Planet Science pages provide topical information on many areas of science and technology, including toxins and pollution, waste disposal and recycling.

http://foe.co.uk
Information about Friends of the Earth and their environmental campaigns, especially on clean-up and waste-reducing issues.

http://www.envirolink.org/
The Envirolink page, a useful "signpost" detailing sources of further information.

http://www.greenpeace.org
Has information about the environmental organization Greenpeace and its activities, including direct action campaigns against dumping wastes at sea, undisclosed radioactive waste sites, and the hazards of toxic wastes.

INDEX

PICTURE ACKNOWLEDGMENTS

Bruce Coleman Collection 40 (John Cancalosi); Forlaget Flachs 35 top (Ole Steen Hansen), 39 (Ole Steen Hansen); Impact *front cover* (Lionel Derimais); Science Photo Library *front cover background* (NASA), 6 (Astrid & Hanns-Frieder Michler), 12 (Alex Bartel), 15 (U.S. Dept of Energy), 21 (Peter Andrews), 22 bottom (Martin Bond), 23 (Martin Bond), 27 top (Simon Fraser), 36 bottom (Hank Morgan); Still Pictures 4 (Ray Pfortner), 5 (Robert Holmgren), 7 (Pierre Gleizes), 8 bottom (Mark Edwards), 11 (Andre Maslennikov), 14 (Thomas Raupach), 17 (Jonathan Kaplan), 19 (John Maier), 20 (Mark Edwards), 22 top (Mark Edwards), 24 (Peter Frischmuth), 25 (Julio Etchart), 26 (Nick Cobbing), 27 bottom (Hartmut Schwarzbach), 28 (Mark Edwards), 29 (Thomas Raupach), 31 (Ray Pfortner), 32 (Julio Etchart), 34 (Richard Choy), 35 bottom (Mark Edwards), 36 top (B Durey), 38 (Mark Edwards), 41 top (Mark Edwards), 42 (Peter Frischmuth), 43 (Hartmut Schwarzbach), 44 (Beldur Netocny), 45 (Peter Frischmuth); Tony Stone Images 8 top (Peter Cade), 10 (John Edwards), 13 (David Woodfall), 16 (Vince Streano), 30, (Jerry Alexander), 33 (Lonny Kalfus), 37 (David Woodfall), 41 bottom (Bruce Forster); Thames Water 18. Graphs and charts by Tim Mayer. Book icons on page 2, the contents page and chapter headings, by Tina Barber.